LETTERS TO LUCA

LETTERS TO
Luca

A personal, in-depth, and over explicit account
of my unrequited love through a collection
of poems, musings and poetic prose

poems by
KAT STRAIN

Letters to Luca
Copyright © 2024 by Kat Strain.

All rights reserved. This book or any portion thereof may not be reproduced or used in any manner whatsoever without the express written permission of the author except for the use of brief quotations in the context of reviews.

ISBN: 978-1-0689109-2-0

Cover design by Rachel Clift.
Book design & layout by Rachel Clift.
rcliftpoetry.com

First printing edition, 2024.

@sistersstrain
sistersstrain.com
The Sisters Strain

I did not know love until I had yours,
    without it—
I fear I shall never know it again.

PROLOGUE

I knew from the first moment I laid eyes on you in your blue sweater, the candlelight flickering across your beautiful face, that I would love you.

That my life had just changed, and I would never be the same.

You gifted me a bottle of rosé and I wanted to weep. The one before you, who claimed to love me, never did as much in nine years. Never looked at me the way you did as our fingers grazed while you handed me the bottle. I doubt you knew what it meant to me. I'll tell you now, it meant the world.

For years I had dreamt of this devastatingly handsome Italian man I would one day stumble upon. He would be charming, romantic, and sweep me off my feet. Fall madly in love with me and take me off to Tuscany to live out my wildest dreams. And here he was! Like I had wished you into existence.

My fated Florentine had me foolishly believing in fairytales.

I was completely intoxicated, hopelessly enthralled. I had never felt such a stirring before. I have yet to since.

Those months together were a dream. The best of my life. For once I felt seen, heard, understood. Like life finally made sense. Like I finally knew what love was and how it should feel. Like I could finally count on something. On someone.

I'd found him, my soulmate, my other half. My future, without a doubt, I saw so clearly in your eyes. In the way they held mine. In the way they sparkled. I was so sure I knew exactly what they said. That they held the same depth of love as my own and always would. I still like to believe they did. Once. For a time anyway.

Yours grew weary and drifted on. Mine never faltered. Were they to rest upon you today, you would feel the same love, hope and adoration emanating from them.

I don't fall easily. When I do it's forever.

Your love for me didn't last the distance and I could never distance my heart of its love for you. Of course, I could never regret meeting you or the memories that followed. Although I have tried to convince myself time and again it would be much easier if I did.

I have forgiven myself for holding on longer than I should have. I have forgiven you for not holding on long enough.

These words all belong to you.

Conceived from your love, your leaving and your lingering effect on my soul. Some pretty, some pitiful. All imperative to the profound process of loving you, losing you, and learning to let you go.

I have collected every letter I have ever written you, Luca. Every poem, every prose, every prayer.

You told me, in that same candlelight at that same bar, the night before you left, that if I ever missed you, I should talk to you. That you would hear me. And so, I did. Three years and a dozen journals. My heart pouring through my pen onto paper. Beseeching you to hear me, hoping somehow you would.

This is how I know it was real. Poignant. Powerful. Your presence filled my life only briefly and yet it can fill these pages with its potency.

In losing you I found my voice. For that I must be grateful.

I hope you read these words and know they are for you. I hope they clearly portray the extent of what you did and will always mean to me. I hope you know how thankful I am for them.

How thankful I am for you... and the ephemeral moments you were mine.

I have presented this collection in the order by which they were written. I ask you to take this journey with me. As my loving and longing grew in intensity and developed over time, so too did my poetic prowess.

I want you to feel each word, each thought and each emotion as I did. Let it build you, bate you and break your heart as it did my own.

Share it with me, so I no longer must carry it alone.

We fell in love as Winter gave way to Spring. Like the snow could not stay to share in the changing season, neither could you.

"How can I leave when I miss you already?"

You asked on the day of your departure - but you did. Mere days after you told me you loved me.

"I would stay if I could."

You caught my face, bringing my averted eyes to yours. I was scared to look into them, scared to believe the promises they held, scared to put stock in the ones pouring from your lips in case you didn't truly mean them.

"I don't know how we will make it work, but we will."

Three months later I would visit you in Italy.

Silent tears spilling on the plane while watching Call Me By Your Name. Terrified our story, like theirs, would end in vain.

  You kissed me twice at the airport and again I couldn't look you in the eyes for fear I'd cry.
"I'm so glad I got to show you all the people and places I love as you are one of them and always will be" and I knew you meant goodbye.

  I wept the entire 12-hour journey home because it wasn't and never could be over for me.

"I know I will wait for him as long as it takes. What scares me and breaks my heart is the fear he won't do the same."

When I need to feel you, I find you here...

My soul soars by the waterfront
Entwined with yours
Connected on every level
True, kind and kindred

Never so open
Never so true
Nothing as pure
As being here with you

Don't want you to leave
Please don't go
Look into my eyes,
My heart will show

You set me on fire
And burn through my veins
Sizzling like live wire
I'll never be the same

This was one of the first poems I shared with you after my visit to Italy. Your hope was hollowing while mine was reaching new heights. You didn't quite understand. You thought it meant I wanted to change who I was for you or to be with you. That was never it. It was about you seeing my fullest potential. The version of myself I could not see before having met you. A recognition of how true and authentic I felt in your presence.

You made me feel I was capable of anything and pushed me to believe the same.

```
I want to spend my life being seen
through your eyes
The woman you see is who I aspire to be

        I'll take this as a pause,
        but not our demise

When I become her, and you become free
Maybe your eyes will come back to me
```

You always asked the sincerest questions
while smoking cigarettes on snowy balconies.

What do you want from me, he said.
Everything
What do you want from me, she asked in kind
I want for you to be mine

I already am.

You are everything I did not know
I wanted and believed could not exist.

Midnight machinations...

```
Your soul sets mine on fire
Your touch leaves my body aching with desire

When I am thinking of you,
Do you think of me too?

Of all the things you wish we could do
And all the ways we should be together?
```

As your correspondence started to dwindle, much like your faith in our future, it became quite heart-wrenching to hold this love for you.

It pains me to love you,
though you've brought me such joy
I despise living without you,
can't shrug it off or be coy
You've changed my world,
in more ways than you know
Despite the distance,
my love continues to grow

It's rampant and wild,
with no sign of ceasing
With each day that passes
its only increasing
I want to tell you every day,
how I long to hear it back
But I know you won't say it,
I'm left in this lack

You're not quite gone,
but not really here either
I wish you'd hold on,
wish you wanted me to keep you

But in the next breath, I'd remember its beauty and become lost all over again.

I love the way you kiss me,
as though you cannot resist
Like it's what you were born to do,
as essential as your next breath

Stealing mine from my lungs,
and suffocating me with its divinity
I require nothing more to exist,
beyond the sweetness of that kiss

Conceived over a candlelit cocktail at Wise Bar reminiscing of evenings we shared there. I sent you a message saying that although I would prefer your company, I felt such comfort in the warmth of our memories. That those memories were enough to keep me full while I must live without you. You said you couldn't agree. That you felt the lack. That it hurt. That you would not and could not do long distance... and suddenly my world turned ice cold.

You are on my mind
Nearly every other thought

Here
Even when you are not

I would not want it
Any other way

For if that's the only place I can keep you
On my mind I hope you to stay

Kat Strain

Hold my heart like you hold my hand
Don't ever let it go

I long to hold you close
To feel your skin next to mine

Breathing with you as one
The thought has me undone

What I wouldn't give for this to be true
To spend just one more day wrapped up in you

You fit me like a favourite sweater. One I could not fathom letting go despite how worn or ratty it gets.

```
Because all your pieces so perfectly fit mine
      This love has got me feeling fine
```

You should recognize this, Luca. The only letter I ever sent to you. All the way from Toronto to Tuscany. A grand and desperate gesture. I often wonder if you kept it....

You're everything
This runs through my mind on repeat
From those words
I hope you never retreat

You might not remember saying them
But I won't soon forget
They still fill me in memory now
With the same weight of what
they meant to me then

Wish I could press replay
To take me back to that day
To all the things you said
And all the things I didn't

If I could have back that beautiful minute
That song, that concert, that dance
I would not squander the chance
To tell you, you are too

Kat Strain

I look at you
And see the face of my future son
That is how I know you are the one

My other half
The missing piece to complete me
The only person who could make my life
all I wish it to be

Because I just want to love you
and I can't
My heart does not stand a chance
living in this loneliness

The sun can shine clear and bright
and warm my skin
But I'll only feel cold and empty within
until you are mine again

Kat Strain

Just looking at your photo
Can break my heart

I love you so completely
Your absence tears me apart

Days may be easier to fake
But the nights are hard to take

Because I want you more than I need my next breath
And living without you leaves me bereft

I crave all the things we haven't yet done
   and dream of the memories we are yet to make.

One day.

I despise its existence but love its promise.

So tragic it is comical. And more than a little crazy... although hindsight suggests you most likely had already started dating your next by this point.

Online
I see you are too
Are you also waiting to see if I come through?
Rereading old messages,
hoping I'll send you something new?
I wish that were the case,
but I doubt it is true

Still, I wait and hope,
reminiscing over you
Wishing I was the person you were talking to
You could not possibly
be doing the same
This behaviour isn't even sane,
but it's what I'm reduced to

Who are you talking to
and why isn't it me?
Why am I so fucking crazy??
Want you calling my line
all the time...
and you're not,
and that kills me

I'll just drink more wine,
pretend I'm fine-
Watch sad movies that make me cry
Go to bed lonely again,
this misery my only friend,
and do it all over
tomorrow

I've got nothing clever to say
even if I wanted to
Feel like I'd be harassing you
You'd respond
to be kind,
but I'm convinced someone new has caught your eye
And I am a fucking fool

Listen to *Cigarettes After Sex*
and weep
Feeling pathetic. Like a creep.
So damn caught up in you,
and you're moving on
to someone new
without me

Check back one more time,
you're still online
Just not talking to me
Why do I torture myself?
In my head I know you are free,
but I don't want you to be
Because I am not

How can you move on to someone new,
when I'm still here holding my breath
until I'm blue

Aching
	with this love for you

Desperately wishing you wanted to
see it through

Kat Strain

So sad and lonely
       In my heart you're the only
              And I cannot have you

I'm losing you,
I can feel it
The tighter I hold,
the further you get
The distance between us hasn't changed,
but you've never felt so far away

Despite this,
my love continues to grow
But now I'm in it alone,
searching for a place to call my home
Unable to find it

Because it's not a place at all
   it's you
And I don't know if you will ever be mine

I
want you
in all the ways I have never wanted another
fearlessly
entirely
void of apprehension or doubt
each day a new torture
having to live without
You

And some moments my sadness consumes me
So heavy, so terribly strong

I am lost if I give into it
so I smile and carry on

But the emptiness remains
It does not dissipate or go away

I am certain to be haunted
until you are mine again, someday

Kat Strain

Another meaningless encounter
Because he's not you

No one does it for me
The way you do

Any other who try to fill the void
Only leave me emptier inside
Because they are not you
And never could be

Kat Strain

The leaves changing colour
a brilliant shade of red
The sun shining upon them
should bring me joy,
but instead

I am lost
in the lack of your presence,
your spirit, your love
Head hung down,
when I should be marveling what's above

I make my laugh sound full so
it will hide my emptiness.

Kat Strain

My smile deceives me
I do not feel as alive as I look
My spark you took
When you left me

I am happy you're happy...

                              I just wish it was with me.

Kat Strain

Nothing remains
My heart still beats but it is not the same
  Without your love
The sun does not shine as bright from above
The air does not smell as sweet

You don't like any of my pictures anymore.
Do you see them?
Do you just ignore?

Kat Strain

I like to think I was fine before I knew you.

Now your absence leaves me feeling nothing but lack.

I don't regret meeting you; I wouldn't take it back.

But you've ruined me.

I relisten to clips you once sent,
because I long to hear your voice.

My mind begs to shut it off,
but my heart makes the choice.

It craves you constantly.

I find you in moments of beauty. The sun warming my face, the breeze blowing through my hair. I feel you everywhere.

Sunshine serenade
spreads joy
across my face
Warming my soul
and filling my heart
Taken by this moment
and lost-

                -in thoughts of you

The days ticked by into weeks and months and I knew you'd let your hope slowly fade. Mine had not ebbed in the slightest of ways.

Lost for now,
but not to be let go

You keep your feelings in,
I let mine show

Too deep to contain,
and continuing to grow

Not a trace on your face,
but written on mine for all to know

Living for the day,
when you finally let me in

When you open to me too,
when your heart I will win

An ode to the chilly mornings we would spend at the park cuddled and content. Sharing music and making plans for the weekend as though those days would never end.

```
The leaves dance
on a crisp autumn day
I'll always remember
moments shared on our bench
this way
```

I did not know just how much I loved you...

                        until I lost you.

Kat Strain

I stare at your photo
Willing for it to come true
For you to materialize before me
For your voice to come through

That is how I'm spending this rainy day
Wondering if you do the same
Do you ever dream of me this way
If you knew I could hear you, what would you say?

Rainy days are the worst,
I mope around
feeling lonely and cursed
Wishing for sun to warm my soul,
for your light and love
to make me feel whole
But the sun does not shine,
              you are not mine,
                          and it is still raining.

Kat Strain

I want your winds to take you,
    wherever you want to be...

                                I just can't help but wish
                                    that place was with me.

I put all my faith in you
Believed your words to be true
But your feelings withered
While mine grew
How could you?

Kat Strain

I need to stop writing about you,
but you're all that passes through
    my mind

Leaving words and lyrics in kind,
deterring me from my effort to find
    some peace

This longing just won't cease,
 it seems you hold a permanent lease
    on my heart

You asked me to, so I set you free,
but forever I am destined to be
    lost in you

Heartsick
So in love, and so alone in it

Kat Strain

You brought light to my life
after a time of deep despair
For that I will always
be grateful to you
You taught me how to love and trust again
In you I found
my hearts truest friend
and soulmate

I try to be all there,
yet part of me is with you
Present myself as whole,
but that is untrue

Kat Strain

I fell asleep thinking of you last night
and you haunted me in the worst way
Terrorizing my mind and body
with thoughts easier concealed in the day

Of all the things I thought we had
the memories we'll never make
The love I thought we shared
and the chances you weren't willing to take

Tossing and turning to my worst fear
for it was only I who loved so deeply
That I will never again hold you near
as you chose to forsake us completely

Relentless and all consuming
persistent the whole night
My heart drained more than my body
upon waking at first light

The terror of the night follows me into day
For it wasn't just a nightmare
Empty and void of you
my heart and arms must stay

Does your chest ache in pain
When you see a photo of my face?
Mine shatters and stops
when I do the same

For yours, my soul weeps
Its other half
Its complete
So lost and deplete
Desperate to unite once again

I think of the boy who told me I was the most uncommon
and unique beauty he had ever seen.
I smile and weep.
"You're not from this planet," he said,
"You make regular beauty look boring."

Several years later, reflecting upon these words,
I added on.

I wonder if he should see me today, as my fleeting
youth slips away, would he think the same?
I wonder if I will ever be seen that way again.

I finally opened myself to another many months after you told me you were doing the same. I did not notice in the dark of night, but the next morning, on my way home, found myself waiting at a bus stop that should take me back in time.

Bus stop blues
Picturing me and you
When you held me here
It's been less than one
But feels like a million years
Since then
Your arms tight and warm
And your breath in my ear
I would trade sunshine
And days bright and clear
To revel in that winter embrace
Once again

it is the kind of deep
dissatisfaction
that comes from repeatedly baring your soul
to another
just to have them turn away

the heartbreak of realizing
their love has swayed
while yours
remains the same

endless, undying, infinite
and unreturned

there is nothing lonelier
there is truly no lonelier a place

I must follow my path
and you must follow yours,
with no idea when
they might meet or cross.

Two wandering souls
unsure how our journeys will unfold,
forced apart but ever connected
our story remains untold.

Kat Strain

What I wouldn't give to find myself
                        lost in you again.

                Only then, did I ever really feel found.

I want to say so much more
To which I know you would not ignore
But I don't know what we are anymore

So, I won't put you out...

Kat Strain

I have cried myself to sleep
More times than naught
The pain of your absence
Leaves my heart truly wrought
And weakened
The days and nights so bleak
Without your presence

Missing your essence
And all that you are
So far from where I am

For my heart, I wish yours bled
As mine does for you

I go out, I have fun and I drink
But still, all I think of is you
Wishing you were the one I was going home to
But instead,
I'll go home alone.

Five months since I have seen your face
Or felt your embrace
~ I am starting to lose the essence of your shine~

I still crave it anyway
Wish for it everyday
~And know I won't be whole until you're mine~

I want you to tell me that you love and
miss me too.

But I know that you won't, you either can't
or you don't.

I wish I knew which one was true.

Kat Strain

I don't think I could realize
my full potential with you
That is why I must be alone so long
So I can come to you whole.

Mind lost in the twinkling lights
Lulling my soul
Saying it will be alright
Don't give up the fight
Believe you will get there, and you will
You'll get your man
You'll get that life
Just trust it
And enjoy the moment

Kat Strain

Only you could still this tortured soul
No way to repair, no way to console
The damage done since you said goodbye
I will never understand why

How you could say the things you have said
Or do the things you have done
For me it truly wasn't just fun

You lifted my heart from despair to enlightenment
These feelings can't just be a fragment
Of my imagination
I have to believe with solitude and observation
You will discover the same

I want to tell you,
but I can't

So I write here instead

That I miss you,
and I love you

It's impossible for me to pretend
Or be like you and play it cool,
I am a hopeless fool

Kat Strain

All the words I want to say
Just wither and fall away
Because you don't want to hear them
And I don't want to upset you

You have made yourself clear
I understand and won't stray
Even though I feel them everyday
And want to scream them at you

Tell you my love is so true
And I wish it were returned
If only you were as bold as me
Could let this flow, let us be free
To see where it goes
And what we could be
To not cower out of fear
And hold my heart ever near

My bed feels empty without your presence...
but not as empty as my heart with your silence

Kat Strain

Basking in your light
I have found my own
despite your absence
it continues to grow
when we meet again
I am sure it will show
without a doubt
in your heart
you will know
It was because of you

I long to know what your day is like
If you miss me at night
Or wonder about mine too

Tears in my poetry book
Listening to that song
Wishing you were listening along

And feeling what I do

Still so caught up in you
With no way to get through
To your heart

Or make it beat for me again

Cry and write instead
Daydream of the days when
I had your love

And you wanted mine too

I'll change the tune
And try to move on
But you're never very far or ever fully gone

From my mind

The way our lips and bodies connect
I know I've found in you my twin
One soul
Two separate bodies
Destined to unite once again

Until then...

Take good care of the other half of my heart

As my move to California swiftly approached and you finalized your plans for Indonesia, I had to accept I must leave this behind to move forward...

I can't wait to leave this city
For the haunting to be through
I only knew you here three full moons
Yet somehow, everywhere
Reminds me of you

I don't want to be free
From the memory of you
But you consume me
 When I let you in

I'll pack you away in my heart
 Tightly
So happy and whole
I can learn to be on my own

I'll visit you there
 Periodically
Until you return to me
Until you are home

Kat Strain

I am building a life
I hope you'll want to share
Can you still feel me?
Though I'm so far from there

What I wouldn't do
To have you near me
My heart still calls to you
Can you hear me?

Does yours call me too?

If it does,
It's not coming through these days
I still yearn for all the ways
We used to speak the same language

United, as one
Two hearts that beat

When separate
 So undone

But together
They complete
One soul

Kat Strain

When you sleep do you dream of me
Is it my face you see upon first waking?

Does the memory of us quench the thirst that drives you
Fuel the spirit that enlivens you

Set your soul free?

It does for me...in the best and worst way

yours
is the only nothing
that means everything
to me
and
only you
can break my heart
like you do
without even trying

Kat Strain

You've got me love-sick.
You were so quick to toss me aside,
while I'm still paralyzed
by the light I saw in your eyes,
when you first looked at me.

Why'd you set me free?

I'll let you go... but I don't know
how to be me anymore
without the hope of you.

A song I wrote sometime in LA, 2019. Sitting under the moonlight, drinking, smoking, and thinking of you...

Do you look up at the stars
On your side of the world
And think of me?

And when your sun rises
Over paradise
Is it my face you see?

You're half a world away
But baby that face
Still consumes me

If I had my way
From your love I'd never stray
Or choose to be free

> So won't you tell me you love me
> Like you did before
> Cause your kiss and your touch
> Leave me craving more
>
> How I long for you
> No one else will do

Don't turn me away
In your heart I should stay
I'll be good to you
Let me see this through

Just wait for me baby
Don't find someone new

[I would soon find out you already had]

After all these months apart
I still feel you in my heart
You're a part of me

Though you're on a different path
I'll be here when you get back
That's a guarantee

I'll handle your heart with care
Always treat you fair
Even if we disagree

No matter where you are
I hope you'll think of me
When you look to the sea

[But you were standing beside her, looking at the sea - and I was nowhere near your thoughts]

> So won't you tell me you love me
> Like you did before
> Cause your kiss and your touch
> Leave me craving more
>
> How I long for you
> No one else will do
>
> Don't turn me away
> In your heart I should stay
> I'll be good to you
> Let me see this through
>
> Just wait for me baby
> Don't find someone new

. . .
Oh, won't you wait for me baby
Cause I'll never find someone like you

The second song I wrote days after finding out you had officially moved on. It came to me in a moment of extreme emotion. The words pouring out of my pen like tears from my eyes. Spilling my soul's story. I wrote the first verse, fell asleep and was awoken incessantly throughout the night by the words that needed to escape. By morning, the song had written itself. My heart's pain poetically purged. Turning my sadness and anger into something much prettier.

```
Cause I'm here crying in the dark
While you're enjoying someone else's heart
In your new life

I know it shouldn't hit this hard
You were clear about your cards
But this just don't feel right

If I could only see you now
Maybe I could change your mind somehow
And you'd be holding me tonight
```

Kat Strain

I should just let this go
But in my heart I know
I'll keep holding on with all my might

> You can't let me go and still try to keep me
> You stole my heart now it's time to free me
> Don't keep me hanging on just to appease me

> Yeah, you caught me
> But baby now it's time to release

I really thought that we were meant to be
Your soul had set mine free
It felt like they were intertwined

Still wishing I could call you on the phone
Beg you to come home
I need you by my side

I opened up my heart for you to take
And you tossed it away
You chose to run and hide

All you've done is push me away
Why would I choose to stay?
Why can't I say goodbye?

You can't let me go and still try to keep me
You stole my heart now it's time to free me
Don't keep me hanging on just to appease me

Yeah, you caught me
You caught me, now release

Kat Strain

I have shared my body and brain with many,
      but my heart and soul
          with no other

You have become
the standard by which
I measure all men

They exceed you
in the way they are here and you are not
and lack in all others

Kat Strain

I hate you most
for all the reasons
that I don't
nor could
or would
or
ever will

Because I only want to be seen as beautiful
through your eyes

You're breathtakingly beautiful
But not only for your face or body
Your soul and spirit shine even brighter
Than the dazzle of your surface form

That's what haunts me

I hope someday
You will atone for all the little ways
You have broken my heart

Because I will never not think of you
Or
Stop wondering what might have been

I thought you were my final step...

but it seems, for you,

I was just a steppingstone.

Kat Strain

Nothing has ever made me feel so good or so bad
As having known you, having you in my life

You are both my absolute best and worst of times
And I don't know what to do with it

Hold out hope on the best
Or forsake you for the worst

I wish you would tell me

I know it was real in all the frustrating ways
I can't stop thinking of you
Even when it is done
Despite the countless feeble attempts at
begging myself not to
I just can't shake you

Even hating you is too hard to do.

Only forgiveness could set me free...
                        and I haven't found it yet.

I wrote you songs...you wrote me off.

A spiteful soliloquy spawned by seeing you share a photo of her. A photo of her at that special place we once shared. Where I lounged poolside, listening to Frank Sinatra under the sunshine, and fantasizing a future where I would marry you there...

Do me a favour
And burn that letter
Those words were weightless to you
And I don't mean them anymore

We don't need to settle the score
You were a beautiful lesson I cannot ignore
Even though I had hoped for more
That is all we were

I have written every word
And sung every song I can about you
To my soul I must be true
And move on

This came to me through heavy mourning the day after my 29th birthday. When I asked you why you didn't wish me well and you told me you could not risk what you had with your girlfriend to be a "nice guy" to me. It was exactly the response I needed to fuel the hatred that would get me through the next year without pointlessly pining for you...

```
I'm not saying I was right
maybe you weren't wrong
but what was here
is clearly gone
thank you for the songs
now I'm moving on
```

Too bad I couldn't feign forgetting you for good...

If I could start again
At the beginning
Knowing what I know now
Knowing how miserably we would fail
And how painful losing you would feel
I would still begin again
I would take all the pain and heartache
For the beauty of what was
When we were

The magic of that time
Was worth every tear
And all the anger, hatred, and resentment
That followed
Our fall
Would you begin again with me?
Would you take that leap?
If given the choice
Would you erase or keep the memory?

At times I play "Strawberry Wine"
and sing while I cry...
just so I can feel you.

Sometimes
When I am drunk
And can no longer feel
the hurt you bestowed
I think to write you
Tell you I don't actually hate you
And I hope you are well
Then I wake up
Alone
Knowing you are happy without me
And I hate you all over

They say hate cannot exist
where love does not also
So, despite my best efforts,
I guess I'm still not quite over you

...that makes me hate you all the more

Kat Strain

Just when I think I'm finally over you,

You invade my mind and meddle with my soul.

Those rare and lonely LA rains hit the heart
a little harder...

```
Red wine, rain, and remnants of you
       Flowing though my veins

I am either drunk or foolish enough
            to believe
     That when the bottle dries and
         the showers cease

  So too might my longing for you
```

Kat Strain

And maybe I don't miss you,
I just miss the way it felt...

    You were the last person to hold my heart
    and the only time I've truly known love

My first ever stream of consciousness poetic prose, conceived on your birthday, July 8, 2020. I swore off reaching out after you snubbed me the previous year and I swear I was haunted by your soul at a pit stop hike in Lake Tahoe.

Just when I think I'm finally and fully over you, you rush back into my blood, and I am consumed. Helpless and overcome. It haunts me if I give into it. It is exhausting to try and resist. You scoundrel. You gave up my body but maintain your stake over my brain. All at once, without warning, you crash into my conscience and my fool heart and weak romantic soul are lost in the beauty of your memory, our love, that time, and the devastation it left in its destruction.

I have said all these words before, felt all these feelings time and again. Shut them out and turned them off. Pretended for a time they did not exist or lost their meaning. Lost their weight. But if I am really, truly, honest, they never will. They are always there, in the back of my mind. Dancing on the tip of my tongue. Itching to be validated, realized, heard. Reminding me of all the things I wish for so desperately and cannot have. Teasing me with their promise and shaming me with their existence and the deep knowledge that they do not matter to you and never will. That they never did. That they did

not matter enough. I did not matter enough.
That I will never, truly, matter enough.
For anyone.

I am simultaneously bored of this sentiment while
also relying on it to feed and strengthen my
soul in some way. I've become senseless. I wish
I could shed this skin and start anew and not
rely on you for anything...not even sadness.
More especially, for the understanding of love
and loss.
The most beautiful blessing and cruelest curse
you could have bestowed upon me.

Do you carry me at all? Even as the faintest hum
in your blood as it passes through your veins and
pumps into the heart that now beats for someone
else. Someone better. Someone who is all the
things you wanted. All the things I could not be.
Are you ever bothered by my memory?
Do I ever haunt you like you haunt me?

I will never comprehend how easily you were able
to discard me. How quickly you could move onto
her and set me free.

        Happy 31st birthday, Luca.

The last song I'll ever write about you...
(which was a beautiful lie)

Wanted you to be
All that I would ever need
The harder I held on, the easier it seemed
for you to set me free

I gave all of me
You left me with your memory
Loving you was easy when
I didn't know how soon goodbye would be

I've picked up every piece
I found the stronger parts of me
I don't have your love, but learning
to love me was the best form of release

I'll move on just fine
Know that I can take my time
You might linger on my mind, but it's time
to leave the past behind

They say you heal in time
You're still a burden on this heart of mine
Tell me baby, did you find someone
with which your souls entwined

Kat Strain

There's no way to rewind
So I'll take these wounds and make them rhyme
Sing them till I'm realigned,
and I finally feel some peace

When will I finally feel some peace?

And then, out of the blue, you liked a couple photos on my Instagram and suddenly I was lost again...ever playing your eager fool.

Some people say love is a choice
One you must make every day
I'd have to disagree

My heart never chose this love for you
It was thrust upon me and somehow remains
Building all the time
Even though we are now estranged

The more I try to fight it, the stronger it gets

Some days I despise it
While others
My heart is only too happy
to serve this life sentence

And if the choice were mine
I'd love to say it wouldn't be you
But every ounce of my being
knows that is untrue

Despite all the heartache and misery
My soul needs you

Kat Strain

>For you were, are, and always will be
>My best
>And most beloved
>Muse

The more I try to forget you
The more I find you in my poetry
Tucked into the deep, dark corners of my mind

A dim but ever flickering flame
I was sure I had extinguished long ago

My head may be great at pretending
But my heart cannot ignore your soft glow
It is the only light it has ever known

You keep popping up lately in everything I do. Triggered by the simplest word or thought. Are you playing some trickery on me from your side of the world? Are you finding the same companionship in my memory? I wish there were a way to know, but maybe this is only a game I play alone. Now that I have opened the floodgates where you are concerned (after keeping them so securely sealed so long) I cannot seem to close them. I have a slight fear of losing myself to the onslaught. It is a fine line I walk. Teasing my senses with the romance of your memory while desperately trying to keep my footing. I cannot afford to be consumed again. I'm certain I wouldn't survive it.

  I also have no wish to lock you back in the box of denial in which you were concealed for so long. What's a girl to do really? Always a little lost...with or without you. Are you here to stay or just passing through? All these questions and no answers. They are irrelevant now, but maybe someday they will reveal themselves.

Until then...

I do so enjoy the way you move through my mind.
Sometimes soft and languid, others heavy and
erratic. Sashaying over my sensitivities and
pirouetting through my pain so seductively, I
have no choice but to join you. I have never
been one to decline a dance and I did always
find in you my perfect partner. It is against
my nature, but perhaps this time I will let you
take the lead. Twist and twirl me through this
tumultuous tango and trust you
not to step on my toes.

I sent you this poem and it opened a can of worms for me. I had moved back to Toronto and was suddenly consumed by your memory. Like peeling open an old wound I was once again lost in the possibilities. Your kind and clever correspondence taken for more, building the assumption you might feel the same as me.

If I saw you again, would it feel the same?
Would it quicken my pulse, stir the blood in my veins?
Could we pick up where we left, or would we have to start all over again?
And if you knew me now, would you call me a friend?
Would any love remain, or has time and distance brought it to an end?
If we could have it all back, would you think twice or dive in?

I've shed my skin so many times I hardly recognize myself
And I don't know the man you are today
But I do know this...
The girl I used to be is still madly in love with the boy you were then
Even if they no longer exist

She always will be

You responded and our conversation was light and cathartic. "Ciao Kat. These are very beautiful words, they warmed up this cold Tuesday afternoon in Pietrasanta and brought back wonderful memories… If we met again somewhere I would definitely love to sit down and catch up, and get to know the woman you have become…"

My heart could not help but be filled with foolish notions and my head with daydreams of arranging that "somewhere", sometime soon. To find out once and for all if I've been holding on to a pipe dream or if there would be no denying, once in each other's presence, the fierce love and passion I've felt certain would remain between us.

Kat Strain

There are no lengths I wouldn't travel
                         to see this through.

I'd even meet you in hell if you asked me to.

I can't say if we're forever
but I know we aren't yet done.

I hope you read my words and wonder
if they're for you.
They are, every one.
Does it break your heart
To know you've left me so blue?
I know you still think of me,
Do you still love me too?

Kat Strain

Let me of any blood that flows through my veins
still humming your name.

I still believe I will one day hold in my hands
all the dreams held in my heart.

That includes you.

A brief conversation about the lack of sunsets you had been experiencing in Tuscany and these words formed themselves.

I have always felt more akin to the moon
How she waxes and wanes
The softness of her gentle glow
Sometimes baring it all, others hardly to show

But there is nothing I would not do for you

If it's sun you want,
I'll set your skies ablaze
Shine bold and bright and fill your days
Lower soft and slow in the evening
Do my best to take your breath away
Give you my most brilliant colours
Cascade them in striking ways

Leave you no day void of beauty
And cherish the opportunity
To rise and set
And be your sun for all eternity

Do you think of me as often as I think of you? If you don't know, it's a lot. It comes and goes in waves. Varying in intensity.

I've tried to convince myself to forget you a million times before, maybe every other thought during an onslaught... but to no avail. No matter the intensity, a banging drum shaking my core or a numb buzz rattling softly through my bones, you are never far from my mind.

How simple and easy things might be if I were able to shut you off, shut you out and forget you.

"No rest for the wicked" they say, so I must be downright sinister. Constantly exhausted from replaying your memory in my mind. Trying to convince my heart you no longer affect me, cause it to quicken and ache, and cursing myself for the blatant fact that you clearly do, so completely.

Damn you and that little taste of such good love you gave so fleetingly. I fear I may one day starve trying to feed my soul with the mere morsels left of it and the foolish hope you may one day toss a few more scraps my way. Maybe there is no other way to extinguish this flame.

So smother me, please? Won't you?

Put me out of this misery.

Take away any lingering shadow of hope I could possibly cling to and let me sink to the bottom of this ocean my tears have built in your honour.

Will nothing else ever satisfy me again?

It infuriates me to feel like an errant toddler. Unable to fathom no for an answer but rather stomp and cry and pull my ears in desperate attempts to coax from you the words I long to hear. That you love me, that you want me, that you would give or do anything to be with me.

That you feel the same.

But you don't and you won't or if you do you won't tell me and I'm lost in the frustration of having no clarity on which is true and no way of deciphering. These questions constantly circulating. Building and building in pressure until I urge to scream or pull my hair out. Then swallowed again in resignation.

No release. No relief.

If love were to find me again, in someone new, would it cleanse my palate? Quell this craving at last? Do I only still yearn so fiercely for not having yet been blessed with the sweet serenity of another? Would your ghost then pale in comparison? Slowly fade away.

Or are our souls only lucky enough to enjoy but one such devastatingly enthralling encounter in our lifetime?

To have but once and so brief a time been able to taste you, in all your glory, a terrible tease... but in the end worth starving for. A poison I would take again undoubtedly. I'd just pray for a dose large enough to quench this thirst entirely or cure me of it forever.

I must concede to the facts.

This hunger is insatiable, and for it I am willing to burn.

Thoughts that float around my mind in quiet moments before sleep...

It is much easier to be vulnerable
with written word then spoken
My pen finds the words my tongue stumbles over
I can never quite express what is in my heart
through my mouth
But through my pen my soul has no trouble
with clarity
Hear me with your eyes, not your ears
Your ears will never know all that is on my mind
But your eyes surely will
Listen with those and trust everything
they tell you
For they are me, my soul and my heart
Splayed out in the open
Bare, unencumbered, unabashed, unashamed and
unafraid

I never use words lightly
I'd never allow them out of my body unless I meant
them with all my being

Lips easily carry lies
Through them words are given carelessly
Gone the second after they are uttered

But on paper words are eternal
Their weight carried forever

Never forgotten

I only write what I feel enough to mean forever
I will write every word I know, in every possible
way, to tell you the extent of my love for you

And pray you hear them
Believe them
And one day return them
Unencumbered, unabashed, unashamed and unafraid
Mean them enough to seal them in ink

Write me your heart, let me hold it forever
You already have mine

Melancholy musings...

Today I feel lovesick, and I cannot pretend it isn't your fault. I want you, need you and miss you. I cannot even sleep you away.

Maybe it's the hangover. I washed you down with too much wine yesterday. Maybe I'm just so damn sick of burning with this fever for you.

Burn for me baby. Let's burn together.

I have been thinking all day about Quebec. About that tub. What I wouldn't give to be back in it with you. What I would give up to be able to stay in it forever. Held by the water and your warmth and to know love again.

Meet me there.

Let's get married in that little place like the owner suggested. Light candles, sip wine and soak in the beauty of our love for the rest of our lives. If that's all we ever do, I swear it could be enough for me. If I could somehow get myself back in those arms, I'd never let you let me go. Never let you release me. I'd never again wish to be free.

Say I'm yours. Say you'll keep me. You can have me for eternity.

I have no desire to be touched again unless it is by your hand. My lips shall remain closed unless moved by your own. My body belongs to you and longs to be your home.

You speak of my passion, but you took it with you when you left.

I long to feel that alive again. Breath it back into my body. Fill me. Complete me. Wake my bones from this wasted slumber. Ignite my soul and stir this starving beast bubbling below my surface. I have been asleep so long; I hardly remember what it feels like to be awake.

Do you live only half alive starved for a taste of what we shared, or have you felt my passion paralleled by another?

My body yearns for yours. Its memory makes me weep. Perfection. Pure perfection in my palms and they itch to hold you again. They will continue to until I do. Until our bodies unite. Until my passion is restored, and this beast can breathe again.
Have no doubt she will consume us both.

And I for one, will be only too eager to submit.

We had a fun little conversation one evening after you reacted to a story of mine on Instagram. For once, you reached out and opened the line of communication. I was drunk off it. But then it leads to this...

Where are you?
Where have you been?

Every day that I don't see your name I lose more of myself.
I'd like to say I don't.
I'm strong, I'm wise, I'm resilient.
Nothing could hold me back.

But honestly, I spend a fraction of every day holding my breath to see if your name appears.

I wish I was better than that.
I say I'm better than that, that I hold my breath for no man.
But there's just no way around it.

I have always and I will always look for your name, and my mood will be based around it.

The control you still seem to have over me is astounding.

It makes no sense.
I am no silly, stupid girl.

Why do you still run rank over my heart?

How?
I'd laugh at me if I saw me.
I'd talk behind my back and whisper about how fucking foolish I am for wanting you and believing you may one day admit you want me too.

I see me, you and the beautiful countryside.
The life we could have.
Should have...let's have it!
Let's build it.
Say yes and I am in.

For once, please my love, promise me beyond what you know you can deliver.
You're not sure.
That's okay, I am.
I'll be the port in the storm.
I'll be the trough line.

I'll be everything you never imagined.

Even with these words, you will never know how
many times I have wished you wanted me the way I
want you. Or that your heart still skips a beat
when you think of me too. That nothing or no one
could ever replace or outdo what you once felt
for me. Because I felt it too.

Only I still do.

It is beautiful and tragic; this pull I feel
towards you. Like no matter the distance apart
or years between, I will always be tethered to
you. And no matter what I do, I cannot shake you.
You are the best and worst thing to ever happen
to me. Even for the pain I am grateful. I must be.
For it is worth the startling streak of beauty we
once were. A blinding spark. A lightning strike.
Full of hope, promise. Full. Before wariness
crept in and spoiled it all as fast as it started.
Though, it was brilliant.
We were brilliant.

I was never grasped by the fickle hand of doubt.
It never sunk its fingers into my flesh. Maybe I
am foolish, maybe it is fated. Maybe both.
Either way it's unfaltering.

I still smile at our past and dream of our future
as though you never broke my heart or shattered

my soul. As though you never gave so freely and then stole back too abruptly such beautiful words and breathless promises. As though you truly are who I believed you to be. My other half, my souls complete. As though you do and always have loved me the way I thought you did.
The way I loved you. The way I still do.

I would never beg but I do beseech you to love me too. Take away all this uncertainty, the miles and excuses, and make those dreams come true.

Make me yours.

Say you're ours.

Make us brilliant.

Kat Strain

The smell in the air has me thinking of you today.

The crisp aroma of melting snow as it rests on the muddy ground under the bright March sun. Melding with the promise of spring in the air.

It takes me back to when you were here.
When I had you and believed I would keep you.

I feel solace with the snow.
Desperately clinging to the earth that warms beneath it, accomplishing the opposite
of its goal.
It does not want to let go.
Neither do I.

When it floated down from the sky, pure and pristine, to settle where it now sits, discoloured and disenchanting, I'm sure it also thought it might linger there forever.
Radiating beauty.
Cradled by the chill of the breeze.

In March I had you.
Held you in my arms.
We clung to each other like the snow to the grass.
Enjoying the sun and glowing beneath it.
Knowing all too well, eventually,
we too would melt.
Slip slowly from our sweet embrace.

It is March.
And in March, I still had you.

Today I don't.

But the smell of the snow, the warmth of the sun
on my skin, and the space that still stirs hollow
in my soul has me aching to fill the void with
you once again.
To hold you in my arms and shine without
fear of fading.

None of my senses are spared.
Even the slightest savour of the breeze can bring
me back to you.
Like the last icy remains, your memory stubbornly
hangs onto my heart.

For me, every day is March.

And just as quickly as I allowed it to sprout,
the seed of hope shrivels within me.

Small glimpses, that is all I ever get.
Tiny little morsels, anyone could see a reasonable
person would starve on and yet I still
try to feed.
I crave it so, even a speck of a crumb
can give me hope.
And before I know it, I'm out to sea again.
Floating, drifting with ease.
Buoyed by your brief and fickle attention.
Until the storm rolls in and I am desperately
clawing at the surface.
Doing all I can to stay afloat while being pulled
down into the abyss.

And the storm always comes.
It is inevitable.
Your tides shift quicker than the beat of a heart.
Charming one second and callous the next.
Leaving me dizzy and dazed.
Shipwrecked by your seas.
My head warns me not to swim...the waters too
turbulent and I have sunk several times before.
But my heart just cannot resist the chance to
float alongside yours.

My soul is far too deep to settle for wading in
the shallow pools of your affection.
So why am I still soaked and shaken by the wake
of your spite?

I sent you a message hoping to stir a conversation. Our last one was so pleasant, and I desperately craved more. I told you I was in my old neighbourhood in Toronto (where most of our memories were made), coyly comparing it to "returning to the arms of a long-lost lover". You were kind but chaste and it crushed me. It was clear the walls I hoped might be slowly conceding had been reinforced and I'd lost any chance of getting in. I felt fraught with foolishness and raw anger to find myself in this familiar position...

I do not want to love you.

Believe me, it brings me no joy. If I could let it go today and never feel it again I would. I would rather be without it entirely than be in it alone. Each time you slight me it stings just a little bit more. I know my hand will get bitten eventually, yet I still feed the beast.

I cannot help myself.

I had a feeling I shouldn't. I did anyway. Maybe I needed to. To feel your guarded callousness and shut off the hope that started spiraling in me. You were open, briefly. I could feel it. I can always feel it.

And it got the better of me.

I have no regrets. I do not choose this love, but I cannot and will not spite it either. It beats in me for a reason. As such, I will cherish it though it brings me only pain. It would hurt more to feel its stirrings and shut them out. Like living half asleep.

Half alive.

I will not censor my soul. Not for anyone. Not even to spare my own sensitivities. I will willingly hurt my own feelings before I would consider denying them. It is not who I am.

I am all heart.

For better or worse. It is big and boundless and brimming with love for you.
And I think it is brave. To love anyway. To love when there is no guarantee of it being returned.

To love despite knowing it never will be.

I have dimmed my light too many times for too many people. I will never again extinguish any flame my heart holds vigil. Even if it burns me alive. Even if you cannot see it or feel its heat. Even if you can and do not care anyway.

I will not put it out for you, and I will not put it out for the sake of my own pity.

I see and respect the state of your heart, but I will not callous mine for its convenience. I also will not continue to hold it out for you. I prepared myself for the possibility of the final dreaded response. The firm denial of returned feelings or care to continue correspondence. I thought, maybe it is time. Maybe that is what I want.

Maybe that is what I need to finally move on.

You did not say that. Not in so many words, but you did not have to. Your energy says it all. Kind but firm. Which is somehow worse. Shut it down. Retreat. Keep your heart to yourself.

It is not welcome or wanted here.

I will heed that warning though I know, unfortunately, it will do nothing to sway the stirrings in my soul.

And still, I cannot resist. My mind swirls with thoughts of you and I surrender to its siege...

My breath catches at the thought
of our bodies meeting.
Flesh to flesh.
Two souls melding as one.
Wild abandon, completely undone.
Nothing in between, nothing left untouched.

The sweet bliss of it befuddles me.
My heart quickens, pulse racing, and my fingertips buzz, aching to explore you once more.
 As though I can almost feel the electricity your skin exudes as it connects with my own.
We never were without a spark.
Somewhere, in some dimension of the universe, in moments like this I am convinced our souls must be coalescing.
Kissing, caressing, languidly loving and longing for nothing.
Free from the bounds of our bodies and all the barriers between them.
It is almost enough to appease the desire.

To know in some way, they are together.
Reveling in the sweet surrender our bodies can only dream of.

My heart yearns to beat under yours.
To pulse in unison, ignited by our passion, nearly pounding through our skin.
Even our bones would not be able to cage the lust that swells within us.
At least there I can love you the way I long to.

At least there...you let me.

I dreamt of you this morning before waking. You asked me, "could you come to Dubai tomorrow?" And I said yes without hesitation. The rest is vague, but I know I pried for more from you. More specifics about how you felt towards me. You gave me only that question as though that was all I could possibly need to know and asked why I had to make things so complicated.

Then you left. I should have been elated. All I have wanted to hear is you saying you want me with you. But my elation fizzled immediately. I knew there was no way I could go. There's too much for which I have worked too hard to just throw it all away to be with you. Even though I want to so badly.

It felt very intense. It felt real. I was somber upon waking. To know even if you said exactly what I wanted to hear, gave me exactly what I think I want... I would not be able to give up my life to be a part of yours. And maybe, somewhere out there, you do want me back, you do wish I could be with you, but you

know this fact too and that is why you would never ask. Never put me in that position. Never tell me all the things that would bring me only brief joy before realizing I cannot have them.
It was nice to see you anyway, my love. Thank you for the message. The timing is not right. There is just no way.

But I will still hold out hope that might change
one day.

Maybe it was never really you. Maybe all this time it was a feeling I have been holding onto. The way you made me feel. I had never experienced it before and have not again since. Was it that feeling I fell in love with?

Is it just that feeling I miss and desperately crave?
You looked at me and it felt as though I had been seen for the first time. Like what you saw dazzled and amazed you. I watched you fall in love with me, and I fell in love with myself. I so badly wanted to see what you saw through those eyes. I so badly wanted to become the brilliance I saw shining back in them. By comparison, every other glance that has graced my form feels weightless. Empty and lackluster. Ordinary. How can I settle for ordinary when you made me feel like magic? And how can I feel it once more without it reflecting from your eyes.

They have not laid upon me in years, yet their weight is still felt.
If I let you go, would my pen dry of ink? If this heartache for you was no longer the needle guiding the compass of my soul, would I still find poetry? Or are my words only spurred from the misery you left in your wake. In your continual absence and dismissal. In the fresh heartbreak that burns every few months when I am suddenly lost in your memory again. Is this longing the only thing stringing these letters together. Will

anything else ever move me in quite the same way or would it all just go away. Leave me like you left me.

Madly in love and bereft of the only thing that made me feel truly alive.
I have learned I can live without you. I have had to. But I cannot lose my souls language.
I think I am terrified that if I let you go... really let you go, then I will lose the part of me that you awakened. My heart never beat as wildly or broke as hard. I never wrote until you. You gave that voice life, inspired it to speak and now I do not want to shut it up. Even if, to my chagrin, it only ever endlessly and repeatedly screams your name. Even if I spend the rest of my life writing about your unreturned love and the ways in which I long for what will never be.

I cannot lose this too.
What if the only beautiful words I have to write all belong to you.

To the broken bits you left behind.
Then again, how long can I coast on your echo. How long could that possibly feed my soul. How much more poetry could I possibly pull from this pit. Surely the well would run dry at some point. Maybe this voice was only ever ignited to parley this passion. Born of its conception and meant to slowly fizzle away with its demise.

Maybe I should consider myself lucky for its brief affair, much like our own, and let it go gracefully as I should have you.

I have never been good at letting go. I do not find myself affected often. Attached. It is quite rare and so when I do, it overcomes me. It consumes me. It pulls me under its tides, and I am helpless. I cling to it, desperate to keep it tightly in my grasp. Unwavering.
Pain or pleasure, I am all in.

A forever kind of soul in a for now kind of world.
I want to let you go. Let me go. Let this go. And I want to feel that way again. With someone who feels it too. With someone I can love without fear or shame. That I can count on for more than just the way they made me feel. Someone who loves me with the depths in which they make me feel loved. Who sees the same brilliance and does not dare steal his eyes away. I want to write them poetry they will read and return. I want these words to remain, ignited by another.
To rely on you for nothing.

But if without you, there is no poetry... what kind of life would that be.
I do not know how to want without wanting you.
To love without loving you.
To live without longing for you.
What is left beyond that longing?
I fear I might feel even lonelier without it.
I do not want you back.
I know those eyes no longer shine for me.

I just burn to feel that brilliant again.

Easter is always tough, but it hit me harder than expected this year. The photo you took of me on our trip to Quebec three years prior popped up as a memory on my Facebook. That night was the last time I felt in love and alive with someone without questioning their feelings or holding back. That weekend was the best of my life. You left shortly after and slowly started drifting away from me. When July came and I visited you in Italy, I couldn't fully give myself to the moment as I had in that photo. I had to be guarded, to hide the intensity of my feelings like you did. But Quebec was bliss. Both of us all in, caution to the wind...

I wore a red shirt off my shoulder and a smile permanently splayed on my lips.
Had never known such happiness before.
Have never again since.
I could say I was carried away by the music, buzzed on the drink, dazzled by the bright lights... but it was you I was truly lost in.
I'd never been so swept away. Intoxicated by another.

I couldn't get enough, neither could you.
We didn't want the night to end.
Did all we could to make it last forever.
We drank, we danced, we sang.
We stumbled arm in arm to our room to make love
and smoked cigarettes on the roof like the little
fools we were.
Enthralled, enraptured.
Completely in love and not a care
for the consequences.
I look at that photo and think if I could only
live in that moment forever, I'd be happy.
If I could make that memory my eternity, I'd need
for nothing else.
I'd have you and the music and
the magic of that moment.
I could satiate myself on the love I saw
in your eyes alone.
Drinking me in with such passion and promise.
I'd never felt so desirable, so electric,
so alive.
So wanted or needed.
Had never burned with such want or need myself.
If I close my eyes, I can feel it
like it was yesterday.
The pulse of the band, the beating of my heart,
the sweet heat of the whiskey burning
down my throat.

And I can see you, so handsome I want to weep,
eyeing me from across the room.
And I know I will never feel as beautiful or
invincible as I did in that moment, in your eyes.

In that moment, I know I love you in a way I will never love another.

In that moment, I have no doubt you love me too.

Kat Strain

I'm sleepwalking through a memory. No matter what I do, there you are.
There we are...that Easter weekend in Quebec.
I took a walk, and my feet led me to the water.
I was transported to that time.
The bright sun, the brisk breeze. Chilled to the bone but my blood like fire in my veins.

The loneliness of today as fierce as the love I felt then.
It has been years. I don't know why I am so haunted as of late. Why those memories constantly nag me. I'd like to think, deep down, I've worked through it and I'm past it, but these constant assaults seem to prove otherwise.
How dare you taunt me so relentlessly while simultaneously thinking of me not.

While moving on.

Living your life unaffected by these afflictions.

I could feel you today...

I make a promise to myself, and it is broken within a week.
I can't seem to keep the simple contract.
I won't think of you anymore.
I will just stop.
You always find a way to sneak back in, boggle my brain and strum my heart strings.
I go about my day as you casually drift in and out of my consciousness.
Softly, swiftly. Stirring the ever-present questions...

> where are you?
> what are you doing?
> am I also dancing through your mind
> at this moment?

Some days I despise your presence here. Today I don't. It's almost a comfort. A soothing caress of my soul. I'm curious to know if you are off on your next adventure. If you are happy. If you have already met yet another to marvel you and minimize my memory or if I still meddle with your moral as you do mine.
I tell myself I'd be happier without these reminiscent reminders, but the truth is they are so much a part of me now that I think I would feel

Kat Strain

lost without them.

I think I would miss them.
I would miss missing you... were I ever relieved
of the burden.

I've got you under my skin and in every beat of
my heart
I find you in each follicle of hair that flows
from my head and sun birthed freckle that
flecks my face

You are a part of my DNA

As though we were made from the same matter
Cut from the same cloth

Two bodies of one soul

You are my blood and the veins in which
it pulses
My heart and its rhythmic beat

My hands and my feet and every piece in between

I feel you in every pore
You are impossible to ignore

You consume me

You fill me and leave me empty
Inspire and deplete me

Keep me craving for more and begging to be free

Kat Strain

My sand, my sea, and the salty breeze that moves me
My poison and my remedy

I've no hope of getting clean

My sole source of strength and the weakest thing about me
You leave me on my knees

And I'd still choose you if you'd let me

Sometimes,
when I contemplate all the beautifully foolish
words I have written for you, my stomach churns
with chagrin. Briefly, I burn to erase them from
existence. To omit every soft secret my soul
has ever borne and leave behind only the hard
substance-less shell our story became.
But I know I never could.
Your memories grip on my heart slowly slips away
but the words left in its wake will remain forever.
Sad sacred bits of my soul to shine on despite the
sorrow they stir. The spark of contrition they
now carry could never surmount the strength of
conviction through which they were conceived or
poison the purity of their prose.
Only a coward would dim their glow or withhold
them from the world. Foolishness is fleeting
but conceding to cowardice is inconceivable to
me. A far deeper shame than the sharing of such
sensitivities.
Though they now feel fickle and flawed in their
frankness, I will swallow my pride, surrender my
shame, and fearlessly fan their flames like the
little fool I fancy myself.

It is both a blessing and a curse
to know the brilliance of blinding love
I am lucky to have ever been graced by its presence,
but its absence often makes me wish I hadn't
Had I never a taste,
I wouldn't know how truly sweet
How bewilderingly beautiful it is
to bask in its embrace
How startlingly cold and empty it feels
to lose its touch and not know if it will ever return
Had it never wrapped me in its radiance
I'd be unable to miss it,
to crave it so
To hold it is bliss, pure and profound
To feel it leave and long for its renascence
A torture most unkind
Had my heart never felt such heat
it might find warmth in a lesser flame
Had it never held yours,
it might be capable of holding another

Tonight, I got drunk and dreamt you were holding me. My eyes weren't even closed. I just can't help but come back to you. Happy or sad, you are the first one on my mind. The first person I wish I could share my emotions.

If I am honest, I wish for that all the time. But it is worse when I am drunk. When I am sober, I can convince myself that you do not matter, that you do not still run my heart. But drunk, I am defenseless. I am weak.

Here, romanticizing our love, idealizing you, and daydreaming of a universe where you love me the same way I love you, and cannot stop thinking of me too.

And again, I must wonder if I will ever be fucking over you. Will I ever be free from this longing? I know it is pathetic and I still cannot help myself. I want you. I want all of you. Forever.

If you do, if you did, possibly, and it was just distance,
I wish you would give me a chance to show what you
mean to me. What I would do for this love. I would make
it work. However long it took. I wish.

But here I am. Sad little drunk. Foolish girl.
Stupid woman, he does not love you.

Accept it. Cuddle your cats. Go to bed.

Nights like this I want to drink my emotions.
Lose myself in liquid love.

God bless wine.

It is the only thing that will suffice when I am
in this mood.
The only relief.
Get lost in the bottle, so I can find you.

So I can feel you.

So I can blissfully pretend the heat burning
through my veins and warming my bones is yours.
Yes, nights like this, only wine will do.
And even that is a pitiful substitute.

Kat Strain

Emotions burn in me like the sun,
and I have felt them all for you.
Anger, hatred, heartbreak, sorrow-
They cycle through me,
building and ebbing into and out of one another.
Only one remains constant.
Through even the worst of my rage
filled fits in your regard,
love has never swayed,
never faltered.
Sometimes a whisper, others a roar.
Even when I can barely hear it,
I know it is there-
all the years, the tears, the distance,
and still this love lives in me.
It always will.

After years of carrying the candle of a romantic "maybe one day" - a candle you repeatedly toyed with, snuffing out and relighting at your whim - my long overdue questions got their answers.

Three years since we last gazed into each other's eyes, I worked up the courage to tell you point blank, I still loved you. After everything, and against my better judgment, I still could not help but to love you so entirely. You knew I would come to you if it meant we could be together. If that was all that was holding you back. You gave me every excuse as to why it could not work but would admit nothing of your feelings for me.

Only then did I realize I had never demanded the words I needed to be free of you. A clear answer about your feelings and the lack of possibilities for our future. I continued to romanticize them in my mind, continued to carry the candle. Not wanting to push you and giving it time to burn. Scared I would not get the answer I hoped for and feeding myself on the endless maybe hanging in the thousands of miles between us.

I cried before I sent it. I knew it was time, and I knew what response I would get.

"I need to hear you say it." I said, "Tell me you don't love me and never will."

"I do not love you and never will..."

I need to put this in a box and bury it
it can no longer hold space in my heart
it no longer deserves to
it is cleansing almost
freeing
to finally have the answers to the questions
that burned at my soul
the waiting, the wondering, the wishing
and hoping
it is all over now
it no longer serves me
it is nothing I wanted to hear
but everything I needed to
now maybe I can finally be free of you
free to fall in love with someone new

My heart has held onto this for so long that it hardly knows how to let go- how to move on. My mind's unsure of what to do with all this free time and space.
This love has gripped me so long, I no longer remember how I felt before. Cannot recall a time when it wasn't tearing at my heart and searing my soul. This freedom is foreign to me. It's alien.

It's uncomfortable.
I want to bury it and be done with it. I am hasty to no longer feel the weight of its shame and sorrow. I want to feel good, happy-as confident and carefree as I did mere moments before this love found me and set me aflame. As vibrant as I felt in its embrace.

Before it left me.
These embers have been flickering for three years and won't burn out overnight. But damn I am done with it. I am angry at the amount of undeserved time and energy I have given keeping it alive. Stoking the fire, believing in its flame.

Convinced it was warranted and worthwhile.
I look forward to the day I no longer think of it. To be fully and finally free. To breathe deeply into my body and not feel the slightest stirring of your ghost. To shed my last tear at your expense.

To never again see your face in my mind
when I think of love or dream of my future.
I need to leave this here.
I need it to leave me.
Completely.

EPILOGUE

I find myself ready to open to something new. Something that could be beautiful. It excites me. But I need to bequeath you from my bones. I cannot carry your ghost and embrace the soul of another at the same time.

My heart is big, but it can only beat for one. I no longer wish to starve, and you cannot and will not feed me.
I had to love and lose you to find myself.

For that I will be eternally grateful.

You breathed life back into my body, pieced together the remains of my shattered heart and brought me light in the depths of a most decrepit darkness. You saw me in a way no other had and taught me how to see myself. You believed in me and replenished my faith when I thought I had lost it all.

Loved me when I was sure I was unlovable.

But most of all, you brought me poetry. The most beautiful blessing ever bestowed upon me. For that I can never express how thankful I am. I have written every word I can think of to try.
Thank you for building me up, breaking me open and forcing me to blossom.

I will always love you Luca...

but you'll get no more letters from me.

ABOUT THE AUTHOR

I have always had a passion for expression and storytelling. First through dance, then performance- on stage and on screen.
Sharing, emoting and evoking feeling in others stirs my soul.

Those mediums allowed me to share the stories and voices of others.

Writing has become a way for me to find and strengthen my own voice and share my stories.
 It is not a choice, but a compulsion.
As natural and essential as breathing.

I feel the urge and I let my pen flow. I never know where or when it might consume me. Sometimes I'm not even sure whose words they are and if they are indeed of my own heart.

Regardless, I am an eager and grateful conduit.

I am a highly passionate, overly sensitive, hopeless romantic brimming with thoughts and emotions and a deep, desperate need to purge them.

Were I to swallow them down, ignoring their urge and denying myself their release into the world, I'm quite convinced I might just burst.

Poetry is both my salvation and damnation. My biggest strength and surest weakness.
 My shameful sorrow and purest joy.

Every particle that beats within my skin brought to the surface,

My pulse, my heart...my soul's true purpose.

www.ingramcontent.com/pod-product-compliance
Lightning Source LLC
Chambersburg PA
CBHW020736020526
44118CB00033B/1019